Sketch Thinking
Sketch (for Design) Thinking
3rd Edition
ISBN-13: 978-1522774549

Introduction 'Some people need to sketch to think'. 4

Chapter 1 How to Sketch 7

    [Tools 01] What happens when you sketch better? 9

    [Tools 02] What is the best sketching tool? 11

    [Tools 03] Why felt pen is better than ball pen? 13

    [Tip 01] How to sketch people? 15

    [Tip 02] How to draw star man 17

    [Tip 03] Star man versatility 19

    [Storytelling 01] Why do you need a sketching vocabulary? 21

    [Storytelling 02] Use space for commas 23

    [Storytelling 03] Containers for ideas 25

    [Storytelling 04] Creating flow 27

    [Tip 04] Head elevation vs. age 29

    [Group Activity 01] Draw the largest crowd you can 31

    [Tip 05] Sketching moods using the eyes 33

    [Tip 06] Drawing age using of eye & mouth 35

    [Tip 07] Use eye-mouth separation to express age 37

    [Tip 08] Use the lips to express a range of feelings 41

    [Group Activity 02] Building a graphic vocabulary 43

    [Group Activity 03] Teach to share by forcing people to steal 45

    [Group Activity 04] Test your storification skills 47

    [Tip 09] Sketch "Cold" 53

    [Tip 10] Sketch "Music" 55

    [Tip 11] Use body language to express feelings 57

    [Tip 12] Sketch "Defeat" 59

    [Tip 13] Sketch "Victory!" 61

    [Group Activity 05] How to gain confidence? 63

[Group Activity 06] Draw a house 65

Chapter 2 How to make your Sketch 'pop' 67

[Tools 04] Tools for mid-size meetings 69

[Tip 14] How to 'jazz' things up 71

[Tools 05] Why pros use chisel markers? 73

[Tip 15] How to make containers 'POP'? 75

[Tip 16] How to express gender? 77

[Group Activity 07] [Tip 17] How to create buzz? 79

[Tip 18] How to make lists readable? 81

[Tip 19] How to draw attractive titles? 83

[Tip 20] How to draw a happy team? 85

[Tip 21] How to draw a timeline?. 87

Chapter 3 Layouts 89

[Tip 22] Create a 'partie' 91

[Tip 23] Avoid dead zones 93

[Tip 24] Influence of layout on group IQ 95

[Tip 25] The ideo layout 97

[Tip 26] Designate a room master 99

[Tools 06] How to stop the show 101

Introduction

Why this Book?

You've probably heard about Design Thinking before — the collaboration method that enables teams of people to achieve high group IQ. In 2011, the University we work at let us offer an innovative course: Design Thinking. I was lucky. The syllabus we made became indexed by Google. In the following months, we were invited to give workshops at Apple, Dubai Electricity & Water Authority, CEDIM MBI program in Mexico DF and at Bielefeld University in Germany.

But then we hit a wall

However, soon enough we realized a frustrating yet recurring failure: no matter how awesome the participants were. No matter how good the team was. If they had no sketch fluency the workshop would not exactly succeed. This was particularly true in the case of engineers that possessed deep technical skills but who never had the chance to attend a sketching course. So, what? What has sketching to do with a workshop's creative output? — You might ask. Everything!— I say. Let me explain.

A Design Thinking workshop is based on brainstorming ideas and then sharing them so they can be improved by people with different perspectives than yours. This happens when an idea hops from a brain to another brain. While hopping brains, an idea might meet other ideas and improve. This is how genius ideas and Aha! moments happen in a workshop. Design Thinking fosters this activity by using a lot of sticky notes. A biologist would call such process 'sticky notes' based evolution. (We call it Design Thinking because it is fancier). So, what happens when workshop participants (like myself) can't sketch at all?

Failure

I am at a workshop. I have this great idea. I sketch it and then, when time comes to share... the sketch is an incomprehensible doodle that no one can grasp. Communication fail→ Workshop fail.

The Solution

The obvious solution to this problem is to teach people to sketch before the workshop! But who has the time to learn to sketch? Another alternative is to enroll on an illustration course. However, even in the case you became a pro at product illustration or drawing manga, those skills help but are not exactly what is needed for a Design Thinking workshop. A different, direct and leaner approach to sketching that did not require hours of training was needed. After months of searching, talking to art professors and ensuing despair, we finally saw the light during the summer of 2015. After a morning hike in Woodside's Wunderlich park, we popped in the d.School hall, there, a woman in white —Alli McKee— was conducting a pilot workshop about 'Glyphs'. This book is largely inspired by her workshop and we are deeply grateful to her.

What is Sketch Thinking?

The term is short for Sketch (for Design) Thinking. What follows is a collection of 36 tips and seven group activities designed to help you build sketching skills specifically targeted to visual communication for workshops. The core principles of Sketch Thinking are: (i) Draw fast, (ii) Sketch 'people feeling something' rather than objects, (iii) Storify your message.

These principles are based on the Design Thinking assumption that the easier the communication, the more creative a group becomes. Therefore, the overarching goal here is how to increase the creativity of your team, also referred to as group IQ (gIQ). Unsurprisingly, in addition to sketching, the gIQ can increase through work on two related fronts:

- making your sketches more appealing (Ch. 2)
- using a seating arrangement that fosters smoother communication (Ch. 3)

Organization

Hence, the text is divided in three chapters:
- Sketching
- Appealing
- Layouts

In addition, to help you navigate the book, you will see pages tagged with [labels]. Four kinds of labels are used to structure cross-chapter functions: [Tools], [Storytelling], [Group Activity], [Tip(s)].

Happy Sketching!
Jose Berengueres, Dubai, March 5, 2017

Chapter 1 How to Sketch

In this chapter, you will learn three things <u>about sketching</u>:
- What tools to use
- The building blocks of sketch-based **storytelling**
- Principles (tips) for **effective** sketching

The goal of this chapter is to become fluent at sketching for effective communication. You will accomplish this through 13 guiding 'principles' or tips on (effective) sketching. In addition, six group activities are included. Finally, the hallmark of the chapter is a storification exercise where you will practice all the tools and principles explained. In this exercise your task will be to summarize a 5-minute TED talk in three Post-It notes.

Chapter organization
This chapter is composed of 26 self-contained units that can be classified in four groups:
- Three tips on sketching tools
- The four building-blocks for sketch-based storytelling
- Thirteen tips for effective sketching
- Six group activities

[Tools 01]

What happens when you sketch better?

In a meeting, often, one can have a group of individuals who taken one by one are brilliant, but that as a group fail in creative terms. Why does this happen? The answer is group IQ (gIQ). Using the creative management process called Design Thinking can help to rise a team's gIQ. How? One of the key steps of Design Thinking is to sketch brainstormed ideas into Post-ItTM, which then are posted on a wall where they mix, combine and compete with other ideas. Experimentally, we know that the more diverse this idea pool is, the better the outcome of the workshop. However, what happens when the participants can't sketch fluently*? What if an idea is sketched but gets unnoticed because the sketch was not appealing**? — In (*) participants' creative energy gets diverted into sketching struggles. In (**) great ideas are ignored because they fail to get noticed. Both events decrease gIQ[1].

This chapter is about gaining sketching fluency so that 100% of your creative energy can be devoted to the thinking process, not the sketching process.

[1] *The five steps of a design thinking workshop are: "1. Gather facts & knowledge, 2. Share facts with team (define), 3. Brainstorm (divergent thinking), 4. Build-on others ideas (convergent thinking), 5. Prototype & iterate". Berengueres, J., 2013. The Brown Book of Design Thinking; UAE University College.*

What happens when you sketch better?

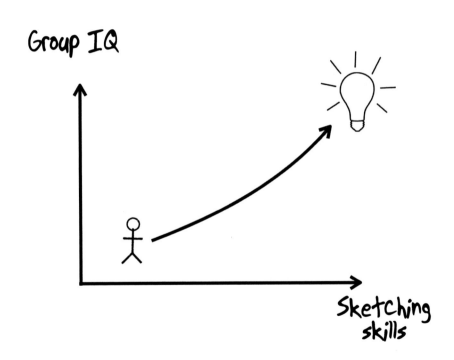

What is the best sketching tool?

The **Sharpie** fine point is the felt tip marker of choice in Design Thinking workshops around the world. Sketches made with Sharpie are visible to distances of up to 1.8 m. In a workshop, this is the typical distance from which people will observe your sketches when they are posted on a wall. The Sharpie fine pen hits a sweet spot: A ball pen produces lines that are too thin to be seen comfortably from a wall (line width<1mm). A thick marker produces lines that are very visible from further distances but that will lack fine detail (line width>5mm).

Alternatives

If you live in a geographic area where the Sharpie brand is not available such as the GCC and MENA regions you can try the Artline ErgoLine Calligaphy Pen 3.0 by ShaChiHata Japan (Ref. ERG-243). This polyester tip marker is water based and therefore the ink is not permanent. However, the Artline's chisel tip is very versatile.

What is the best sketching tool?

Why is felt marker better than pen?

Another advantage of felt tip markers compared to ball pens is the fact that they produce a steadier trace. This is due to the higher lateral friction of the felt tip. A drawback of felt-tip markers is their shorter durability. An efficient ball-pen marker can draw a continuous 2 km long straight line before running out of ink. A typical felt-tip hardly reaches the 500-m mark. The illustration shows a comparison between three different types of drawing tools. **Top**: 10 straight lines drawn with a ball pen. **Middle**: 10 straight lines drawn with a 0.5 mm tip. **Bottom**: 10 straight lines drawn with a felt tip.

The lines are drawn by the same person. The lines start on a point on the left and end up on the right side of the page. Notice how the dispersion of the lines' end points is similar in each case. However, the lines drawn with the felt tip are less wobbly than the lines drawn with the ball pen. This is due to higher (and steadier) friction provided by the comparatively large contact area of the felt tip with the surface.

Why felt pen is better than pen?

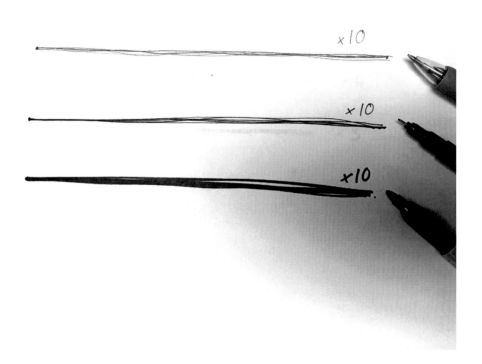

How to sketch people?

In this illustration from left to right we have the stick man, the tooth man, and the star man. As a kid, you probably learnt to draw the stick man. The stick man is an efficient way to sketch a human. However, it is hard the make him express feelings. Enter the star man...

The star man

A very simple way to radically improve the appeal of your sketch is to ditch the stick man and adopt the star man. One drawback of the star man is that it requires ten strokes (stick man requires five strokes). However, as we will see in the next pages, learning to draw the star man will pay off handsomely in terms of communication power.

The tooth man

Between the stick man and the star man we have the tooth man. The tooth man is marvel of efficiency, only three strokes are required. As we will see later the tooth man is best suited to draw quick anonymous crowds. In any case, both he star man and the tooth man are a far more empathic alternative to the stick man.

How to sketch people?

Stick man → Tooth man (good for drawing crowds) → Star man

How to draw the star man

To draw the star man always start with the **shoulders**, then proceed to the limbs clockwise. Finally, draw the head. Play with the curvature of the limbs to express balance, gaze direction, intention direction and other body language attributes. The key to draw the star man is to control the width of the shoulder. The shoulder width should be like the diameter of the head and never much wider than the head.

How to draw star man

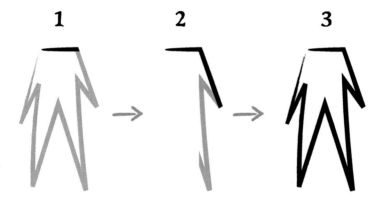

1   2   3

Star man versatility
These three poses exemplify the versatility of the star man.

Left: Neutral position. Notice how both arms are asymmetric. The asymmetry has the purpose to avoid the 'Terminator' effect and give some sense of spontaneity to the figure.

Middle: Pointing star man. Notice how the shifted position of the head totally changes the intention of the figure from neutral to very assertive.

Right: 'Ballet' star man. Notice the difference of width between the thicker right arm and the thinner left arm. This conveys which arm is pointing forward and which arm is pointing backwards. Notice the bend of the legs to convey femininity and lightness of movement.

Star man versatility

neutral   pointing   ballet

Why do you need a sketching vocabulary?

Several authors have pointed elsewhere the effectiveness of storytelling. The best pitches[2], the best commencement speeches[3], and the best arguments all involve good storytelling.

How does storytelling work?

Maybe you never realized but every time we speak we do not think every letter we are going to say, not even every word. All those details are automated allowing us to focus on higher level thinking. However, to sketch a story as fluently as you talk and write, first you will need to build a graphic vocabulary. So, that when you need to visualize someone in a 'happy mood' for instance, you know exactly what to draw quickly and effortlessly without losing your train of thought.

Why build a graphical vocabulary?

In the next pages you will learn the elements to tell a story fluently. We draw a parallel with essay writing. Where in the case of essay writing we tell stories using: (i) words, (ii) sentences, (iii) punctuation and, (iv) paragraphs;   when sketching we will use: (i) symbols for words, (ii) space for comas, (iii) containers for paragraphs and, (iv) arrows for flow. Of the four elements, perhaps the hardest to master is the graphical vocabulary. In the following pages we will show an exercise to gauge your graphic fluency.

[2] *Identity 2.0 Keynote OSCON 2006, Dick Hardt*
[3] *Stanford Commencement Speech 2005, Steve Jobs*

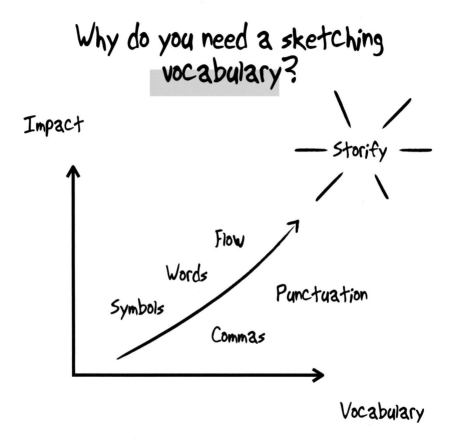

Use space for comas

Frames, containers, space and negative space are the commas and paragraphs of the sketching world. To separate ideas you can use space. To separate two objects visually, use a gap at least half the size of the smaller object. To merge ideas use any smaller gap. Separating ideas with gaps will let you create 'steps' that will enable you to structure your flow. In the illustration two containers A and B are shown. **Top** row: A, and B are clearly separated. **Bottom** row: It is not clear if A, and B are separate ideas because they are close.

Use space for commas

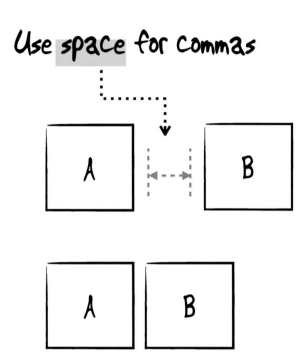

[Storytelling 03]

Containers for ideas

This illustration shows three types of containers for ideas. In a sketch, containers are the equivalent of paragraphs. They can be any shape. Bubbles, squares, circles can function as a container. As in the case of a paragraph, the container function is to agglutinate bits and parts into a unit. Our favorite container is the Post-It because it can be easily pasted, cut, moved and replaced.

Containers for ideas

use containers for paragraphs

Creating flow

Dividing your story into steps can help you structure your story so that it is easier to understand. To connect the steps you can use arrows. Arrows create flow between steps. In a sketch arrows are the equivalent of connective adverbs such as:

- *Firstly,… Secondly,… Thirdly,…*
- *In the beginning,… then,… finally,…*
- *First,… then… after*
- *To start with,… However,…*
- *In the first place,… In the second place,…*

One way to create flow is to connect your containers with arrows. Some authors recommend that you label your containers with numbers too (1,2,3...); even if you think the order flow is obvious, this will help newbies looking at your story for the first time to know where to start[4].

---

[4] *Got a wicked problem? First, tell me how you make toast, TED, Tom Wujec, 2015*

Creating flow

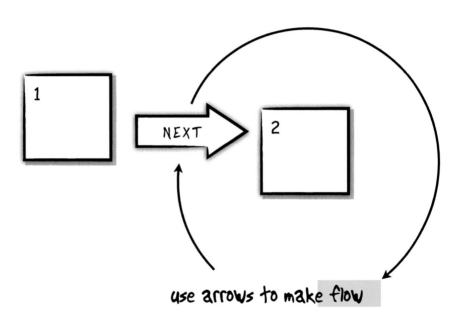

Recap

So far we have seen how to use white space, how to use containers and how to create flow. Following, you will start building your graphic vocabulary. First, you will start with humans, their faces and how to modulate their body language. Then, you will practice how to sketch symbols. Finally, we will ponder how to sketch emotions.

Head elevation vs. age

Now let's revisit our old friend, the tooth man. As we said previously, the tooth man is anonymous in nature and great for crowds, yet it has some tricks up in the sleeves. For example, to modify the age of a tooth man you can use the head elevation. The higher the position of the head (the circle) the younger and more alert your tooth man will appear. The lower the head, the older and wiser your tooth man will appear to be.

Head elevation vs. age

young   old   older

[Group Activity 01]

Exercise: Draw the largest crowd you can (30s)
While the star man is versatile when what you need to draw
is a crowd, the tooth man is a more efficient option (three
strokes).

Instructions
Give each student a blank A4 sheet. Challenge the students
to fill the sheet with a crowd as fast as they can. Time limit:
30 seconds. If you are in a class, you can offer a little prize
such as a candy or Sharpie to the student with the highest
head count in their A4. Though, be warned, once you start
offering prizes some students get stoked!

Exercise: Draw the largest crowd you can (30s)

Sketching mood using the eyes

Eye modulation is a popular way to convey mood in Asia. However, it is an under-used resource in the West.

Left: In the illustration, a happy face can be expressed by painting the eyes as inverted U-eyes.
Middle: The feeling of being crossed can be conveyed using the so-called X-eyes.
Right: A helplessness feeling can be conveyed drawing U-eyes.

Sketching moods using the eyes

happy   cross   hopeless

[Tip 06]

Drawing age using eye & mouth
The distance between eye and mouth can be used to convey age. This illustration shows that the more the eye-mouth gap, the more age.

Drawing age using eye & mouth

toddler ⟶ adult

Use eye-mouth separation to convey age
The illustration shows three different ages. The red line is
shown for comparison purposes.

Left: A face of an eight month toddler.
Middle: A typical kid face.
Right: A face of an adult or young adult.

Use eye-mouth separation to express age

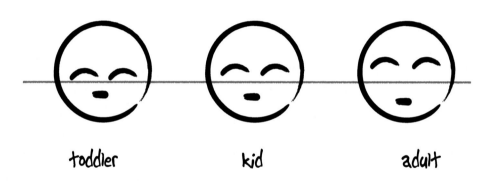

toddler   kid   adult

… except for the grandma case. (Akira Toriyama)

Toddler vs. grandma

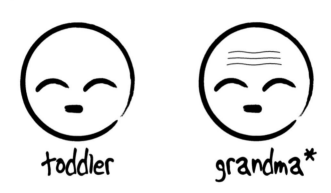

toddler   grandma*

*...except for the grandma case, where proportions
become again those of a toddler – Akira Toriyama

[Tip 08]

Use the lips to express a range of feelings

Lips not only can be used to express the typical happy and sad moods, but also other intermediate moods. Like the eye before, lip modulation is an under used resource in the West. A full range of emotions exists between the archetypical smile (in the illustration, the face labeled 'happy') and the inverted-U ('sad'). Use the lips to express a range of feelings.

Use the lips to express a range of feelings

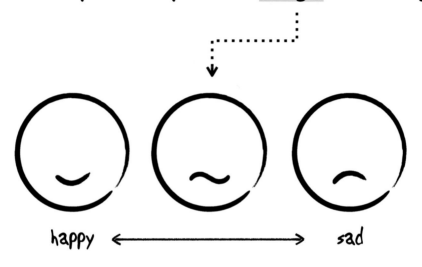

happy ⟷ sad

Building a graphic vocabulary
The purpose of this exercise is to realize how lack of fluency in sketching can distract your thinking. You will notice that most students, specially engineering majors are proficient at sketching objects such as a car or a robot, but struggle when instructed to sketch verbs (or nouns that represent actions), such as communication or affection.

Instructions
This is a rapid fire exercise. Sketch the following words. Allocate eight-seconds to each. List of words to sketch:

1. Love
2. Robot
3. Key
4. Collaboration
5. Communication
6. Flower
7. House
8. Time
9. Summer
10. Cold
11. Hot
12. Hope
13. Athletic
14. Hungry

Exercise: Building a graphic vocabulary

[Group Activity 03]

Teach to share by forcing people to steal

People are wary of stealing. But stealing is OK as long as you give credit. In knowledge intensive organizations such as McKinsey&Co. *stealing* is a metaphor for information sharing. McKinsey's internal case study database for instance, is a source of competitive advantage for its clients[5]. However, many organizations live in a culture of information hoarding, where sharing is seen as a win-lose proposition among competitive employees. This is a great exercise to change the culture of organizations where information sharing is not the norm. A way to make participants get comfortable with *sharing* is by using the guided mastery method[6].

Instructions

Use *guided mastery* to make people more comfortable with the idea of improving their own ideas with foreign ideas.

> **Round 1**. Invent objects. Ask the students to fill a blank sheet with new objects/patterns composed exclusively of straight lines. Share the results.
>
> **Round 2**. Repeat with lines and triangles. Allow them to incorporate one interesting element they might have seen from a peer during the previous round. Share.
>
> **Round 3**.Repeat with lines + triangles + squares. Share final results. Rationale of habit formation: stealing is ok.

[5] Source: McKinsey&Co.
[6] Kelley, T. and Kelley, D., Ch. 8, 2013. *Creative confidence: Unleashing the creative potential within us all*. Crown Business.

Teach to share by forcing people to steal...

[Group Activity 04]

Test your storification skills
Instructions
Summarize a TED talk in three Post-Its. In this exercise you can practice all the previous sketching principles and tips in one single exercise.

Round 1
1. **Watch** Paolo Cardini's TED talk *Forget multitasking, try monotasking* (5 min)
2. **Sketch**. Tell the students to summarize the talk by using three post-its on an A4 sheet (5 min). This is a chance to use containers, flow and spaces
3. **Share** results in pairs (5 min). At the end of each round the participants can check their peers' work and incorporate new elements (steal)
4. **Switch** places. The students switch partners

Round 2
1. Watch the talk again
2. Sketch (*encourage stealing from Round 1 share*)
3. Share (different partner)
4. Switch places again

Round 3
1. Watch the talk again, Sketch and, Share
2. **Reflect**. Post all the A4 on a wall or on the floor making a circle. Observe the different strategies used to summarize the story

Test your storification skills...

1. Watch Paolo Cardini's talk *Forget multitasking, try monotasking*
2. Summarize the talk in three Post-Its

Share & steal from your peers

3. Share (in pairs)
4. Incorporate at least one 'element' from peer (*stealing*)
5. Iterate three times

Final round
Use the "circle" to display each work equally. This is a nice chance to reflect and to provide a spiritual closure to a workshop. Photo by Alli McKee. Workshop at the d.School, 2015.

Sketch 'Cold'

Now that you have practiced the star man, learned the basic elements of sketch-based storytelling, and mastered the art of storification. Lets see few additional tips regarding the sketching emotions, body language, and sketching confidence.

Sketching emotions vs. objects

The illustration shows four ways to sketch cold. Ask the students how would they sketch the word 'cold'. After a few workshops we noticed that each major tends to sketch cold in a particular way but seldom the shivering man. However, when possible, try to sketch emotions — a user feeling something — rather than an abstract or inanimate object.

Sketch "Cold"

1. boring

2. typical

3. impersonal

4. When possible, visualize feelings

[Tip 10]

Sketch 'Music'

When possible, try to sketch experiences rather than icons.
Ask the students: Why do people listen to music? Is it to
keep their ears warm or to *feel* the joy of music? Try to
sketch the joy of music. **Sketching notes:**
-   emotions are human-centered (use a face)
-   use familiar objects (don't make people guess)
-   focus on the outcome of the activity (joy)
-   use support icons to defuse ambiguity (music notes)

Sketch "Music"

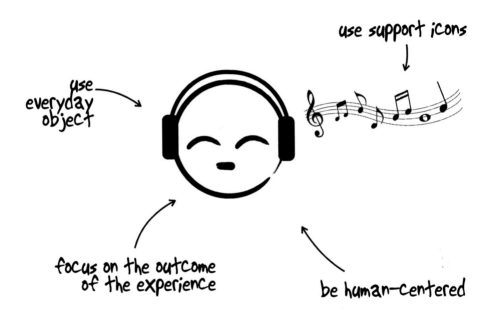

use everyday object

use support icons

focus on the outcome of the experience

be human-centered

[Tip 11]

Use body language to express feelings
After the facial expression, body language is the second best indicator of feelings. A large number of psychologists have pointed that about 80% of communication is nonverbal[7] (with a big component belonging to body language). Only the rest is oral so, Isn't it time you start using more body language in your sketches?

In the illustration,
Left: A neutral star man.
Right: A leaning body to one side and the wiping hand are used to convey distress.

7 Knapp, M.L., Hall, J.A. and Horgan, T.G., 2013. Nonverbal communication in human interaction. Cengage Learning.

Use body language to express feelings

use unbalance to show distress

[Tip 12]

Sketch "Defeat"

When trying to sketch a feeling it is better to over dramatize. The principle of exaggeration is one of the 12 classical principles of good animation used in Disney cartoons and traditional Japanese animation (anime). See also *John Lassetter's "Principles of Good Animation", Siggraph 1987.*

When in doubt, over dramatize

In the illustration three star men are depicted with different levels of exaggeration. Which one communicates the feeling of defeat more effectively?

Left: Neutral star man.
Middle: Star man tilts, wipes face with the hand.
Right: Star man tilts, wipes face with hand, knees down.

Solution: Right

Sketch "Defeat"

neutral ⟶ total loss

Sketch "Victory!"

The figure on the right side is called ***expansive arms***. It is a universal symbol of accomplishment. Even blind people (who have never seen anyone doing this body pose) will spontaneously do this pose when they win a race.

Left: Neutral star man.
Right: Victory pose star man. Notice the head is positioned higher to express expansion. Notice that "Yeah!" has been added to defuse the ambiguity of the pose, which can be also interpreted as "help!" (because the legs are spread.)

Sketch "Victory!"

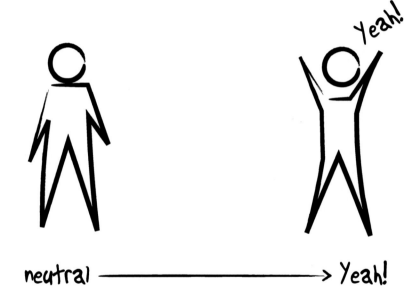

How to gain confidence?

When we arrived in the Valley we didn't know anyone outside of our comfort zone. Cesar and I decided that we would try to make an effort to socialize more with strangers. So every Saturday afternoon we would go to a random Starbucks. We met self-taught illustrator Juan Villa at such a Starbucks near Edgewood. He taught us this hack.

Instructions

Write numbers from 1 to 9. The left hand writes the mirror image of the right hand. Both hands write at the same speed. Most people are ambidextrously good at number sketching. Gain confidence by discovering your hidden abilities. Share your 'mirrors'.

Exercise: How to gain confidence?

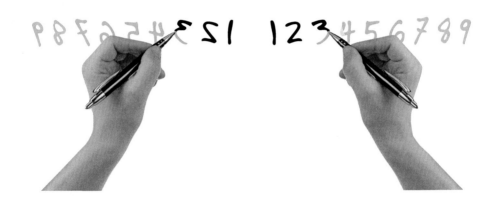

[Group Activity 06]

Draw a house

The purpose of this exercise is to gain confidence through blind scene recall.

Instructions

Close your eyes. With your eyes closed, draw: the horizon line, a house, a path leading to the house and a sun shining in the sky. Now open your eyes. You will be amazed at how accurately you can draw even with your eyes closed. Exercise by Juan Villa (San Mateo).

Exercise: Draw a house

Chapter 2 How to make your sketch 'pop'

In this chapter, you will learn one thing: How to make a sketch more appealing. To accomplish this feat, we will use color, and shading techniques borrowed from the Creative Problem Solving Institute, Buffalo. These were showcased in Dubai by Deborah Madelaine, a packaging innovation engineer at MARS Inc. In this chapter, you will need a chisel marker, (not the Sharpie of chapter 1). A standard option is Mr. Sketch brand. Mr. Sketch is larger than the fine Point Sharpie of Ch. 1, so it is suited to draw on larger surfaces such as an A3 paper or a Flipchart. If you are on A4 do not be afraid to draw larger star men.

Chapter organization
This chapter is composed of ten ideas organized in four topics:
1. **Shades & Color**
2. **Chisel** markers
3. Four **tips** to make a sketch **'pop'**
   - Shading, Jazzing, Container popping, Buzzing
4. Four **templates** for
   - Gender, Banners, Lists, Teams, Timelines

2

Tools for mid-size meetings

A popular sketching surface for mid-sized meetings is the Flipchart. In such cases, 5 mm thick markers work great. You will need two kinds of markers (each of different color): a primary marker, a secondary or accent marker. The primary marker is used for outlines, text and shapes. Effective primary marker colors are black and dark blue. The accent (or secondary marker) is used for shades. Typical accent colors are light colors such as: yellow, orange, light green and pink. Typical primary-accent combinations are: blue-red, black-green and black-orange.

Tools for mid-size meetings

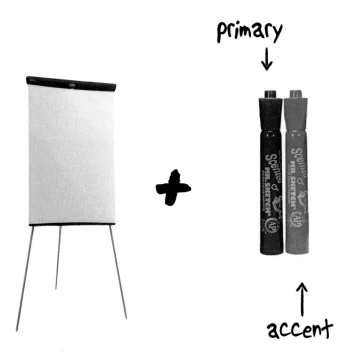

primary ↓

accent ↑

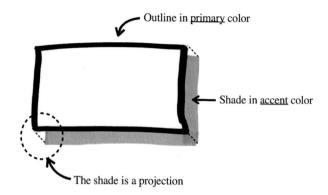

Outline in <u>primary</u> color

Shade in <u>accent</u> color

[Tip 14]

The shade is a projection

How to jazz things up
Basically, there are two ways to make a sketch more appealing: shades and jazz hands (the radial lines).

Shading
Note about shading: the shade never extends to the corner of the object because shades are always projections that result from gaps between two objects. What are the best colors for shading? Light colors. Note that colored shades do not exist in the real world. This is one reason they are so powerful at making outlines 'pop'. Avoid dark colors for shading.

Before-after comparison
The illustration shows two podiums. The one on the right (after) conveys the idea of "winning" significantly more **enthusiastically** than the one the left due to the jazz hands and, the shading (here in a low key grey color). Note that you can add shading to the 'jazz hands' too.

How to 'jazz' things up

Why pros use chisel markers?

Once you used a chisel marker you will not want to go back to isotropic markers like the Sharpie because by rotating a chisel 90 degrees one can instantly change the width of the marker. It is like having two markers in one. Remember when in a workshop, every second counts. Being able to change the width by mere wrist twist saves significant amounts of time.

Why pros use chisel markers?

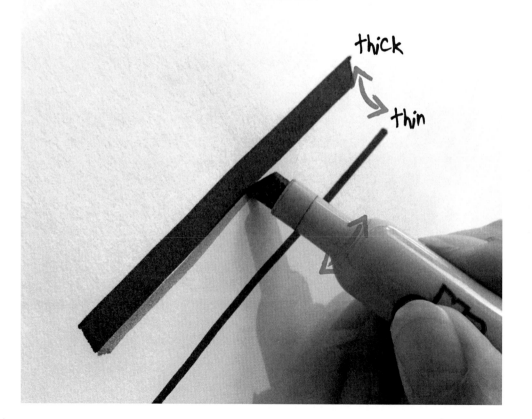

thick

thin

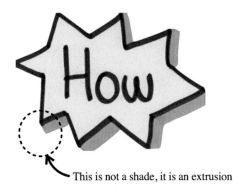

This is not a shade, it is an extrusion

[Tip 15]

How to make containers 'pop'?
The illustration displays an example of 'pop' done with Mr. Sketch. The thin side of a black Mr. Sketch marker was used to draw the outlines of the containers. The wide side of the markers were used to 'shade'.

Shading exception
Note that in this case the shades extend to the vertex of the containers. This is the only exception to the shade projection rule we saw earlier. In fact, these are extrusions rather than shades.

How to make containers 'pop'?

[Tip 16]

How to express gender?

Unfortunately, one can take advantage of gender biased stereotypes to convey gender. Feminine hair style can be used to turn a tooth man into a female and a baseball cap can be used to turn a gender neutral head into a male. Note that use of caps by males is prevalent in some parts of America, but less so in Europe and other countries. A key point of caps is that they help convey gaze direction, an important social cue.

In the illustration,
Left: A cap on a man (stereotype) is used to convey the gender and the gaze direction.
Right: A hair style on a woman (stereotype) is used to convey gender and gaze direction.

Note on hair style stereotypes

The hair style is a powerful tool to convey gender. In addition, some experiments have measured how much hair style influences how a person is perceived. In an experiment in Germany[8], a robot-mannequin with a short hair (male stereotype) was (slightly) rated as more proficient (and less empathetic) than the same robot-mannequin when fitted with long hair.

---

[8] *Eyssel, F. and Hegel, F., 2012. (s) he's got the look: Gender stereotyping of robots. Journal of Applied Social Psychology, 42(9), pp.2213-2230.*

How to express gender?

man   woman

How to create buzz?

Nothing draws more attention than having an already built in crowd looking at something (use caps to convey gaze). Note that you can use smiles to indicate gaze direction too. This sketch combines the **four** techniques we learned so far:

1. Tooth man for crowds
2. Caps/Smiles for gaze
3. Jazz hands for hype
4. Shading to increase appeal

[Group Activity 07]

You can convert this illustration into an exercise. First, draw the Flipchart rectangle. Second, draw the standing man next to it. At this point, ask the audience, how would you create buzz around this salesman? Then you can guide the audience to give you suggestions to be added in sequence. Note how the buzz level increases at each step. Preferred order:

1. Draw the crowd
2. Draw the gaze indicators
3. Draw the jazz hands
4. Add shades

How to create buzz?

[Tip 18]

How to make lists readable?

Using alternate colors can make a dull list (left) more readable (right side). For best results, use two dark tones such as black and dark blue.

How to make lists readable?

Shopping List
- ☑ Milk
- ☑ Pepper
- ☑ Orange Juice
- ☑ Flowers Mama
- ☑ Apple pie
- ☑ Soap

Shopping List
- ☑ Milk
- ☑ Pepper
- ☑ Orange Juice
- ☑ Flowers Mama
- ☑ Apple pie
- ☑ Soap

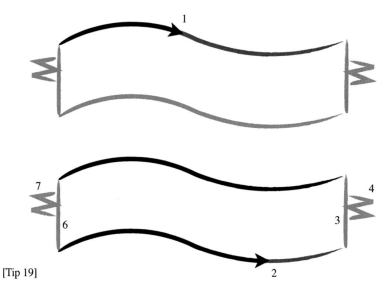

[Tip 19]

How to draw attractive titles?

Instructions to draw the wavy banner. Start with the top wave (1), then the bottom wave (2). If you draw 2 immediately after 1, the motor memory is still fresh and the second wave will be a perfect copy of the first one. Then the side (3), the wing (4), and (6,7). Finally, you can add shades. (Don't forget to add shades to the wings too!)

How to draw attractive titles?

[Tip 20]

How to draw a happy team?

The illustration shows a team/family of three. It is composed of three star men in victory position. The leader figure appears in the center. Two smaller figures are placed on the sides. Note the importance of the caps, signaling that this family members are looking at each other. Finally, no family is complete without a little mascot.

Note on the admirer effect

The little mascot increases the buzz by means of the so-called *admirer effect*. (See also *crowd* in *How to create buzz* in Tip 17)

How to draw a happy team?

[Tip 21]

How to draw a timeline?
The illustration shows a timeline with milestones and a goal.
For the target, usually red color and concentric circles are
used.

Source: Creative Problem Solving Institute.

How to draw a timeline?

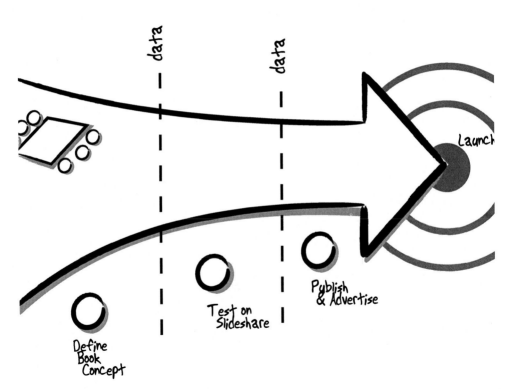

Chapter 3 Layouts

In Ch. 1 we saw how communicate an idea effectively with a sketch. In Ch. 2 we saw how to make that sketch appealing so your good idea gets noticed. Note that a good idea that goes unnoticed is a good as a dead idea. Both skills are critical to increase your group IQ. However, unappealing or poor sketching is not the only enemy of gIQ. In this chapter, we will address another **silent** yet pervasive **killer** of meeting creativity: bad layouts.

Motivation

We decided to add this chapter after attending a leadership training by David Nino where an inflexible room layout hindered the success of the workshop — an offender as common as choosing wrong marker size. A bad layout can kill a meeting's **creativity** in four ways:

1. Lowering the group IQ
2. Hindering communication
3. Fostering distractions
4. Triggering confrontational behaviors

Chapter organization

This chapter is composed of six ideas organized in two topic areas:

1. Physical aspects of **successful** layouts:
2. Room **logistics**

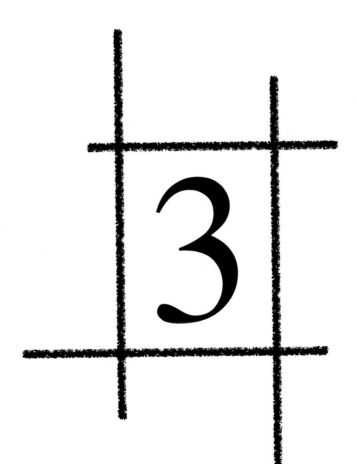

Build a 'partie'

The first thing to consider when setting up a meeting layout is how to **protect** your audience from distractions so that they can focus 100% of their finite attention in the meeting. Distractions can kill meetings. In any meeting the number one source of distraction is the door. That is why upscale theaters and restaurants use curtains to separate the entrance from the seating area.

What is a partie?

A *partie*[9] is a semi-barrier that separates spaces devoted to incompatible activities (such as entering a room /eating food quietly). For example, outdoor restaurants usually separate the terrace where customers eat from pedestrian traffic by using a barrier of plants.

A makeshift partie

An example of how not having a partie can hinder a meeting is the typical classroom. Most are fitted with no partie between the entrance and the seating area. In the worse cases the stage is next to the exit door! In such layouts, anyone exiting or entering the room creates a disruptive event. Nevertheless, even in such bad-design cases you still can do something about it. Create a makeshift partie by placing a movable whiteboard between the door and the seats. The best parties are symbolic ones.

A whiteboard can be used as a makeshift partie.

[9] *Frederick, M., 2007. 101 things I learned in architecture school. Cambridge: Mit Press.*

Build a 'partie'

distraction-proof area

Entrance

Dead zones

A dead zone is where information does not reach clearly
Avoiding dead zones is difficult in N>10 teams. Dead zones
can occur visually but also in spoken communication. They
can also occur in terms of physical interaction if "thinking
with the hands" is required and some participants cannot
reach the "play" area.

Reach: 3.0m / 20 ppl

Visual dead zones

The thicker the marker, the longer its reach. A sketch made
with Sharpie fine pen has a reach of 1.8 meters. This means
that you can reach at most four to five people
simultaneously. On the other hand, a 5 mm marker can be
seen from a distance of 3 meters. This means you can reach
anywhere from five to twenty people simultaneously.
Choose the marker size that suits your team size. In
addition, note that smaller tables feel cramped, but lead to
less dead zones.

Reach: 1.8m / 5 ppl

Audio dead zones

Similarly, in a noisy place such as a restaurant, the lauder
the background noise, the nearer people need to be to you
to hear your voice. For every 3 dB increase in ambient
noise, you will need to double your volume to reach the
same people with the same clarity. A sign of a good
meeting room is low background noise. The background
noise level usually found in offices and restaurants means
that meetings of more than eight people are not realistic in
such venues, as the dead zone will encompass too many
participants.

Avoid dead zones

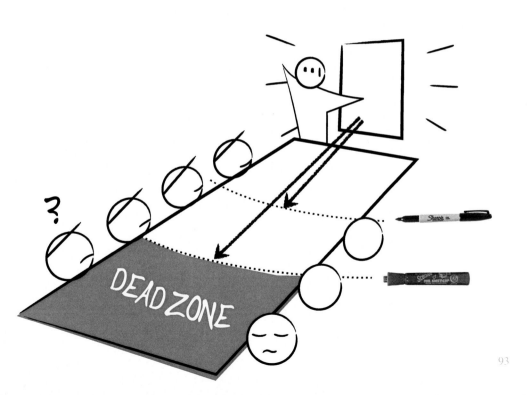

The wedding table. The balls represent heads of people seating. This layout **maximizes** confrontation risk between parties sitting across. The large table diameter (2.0 m) hinders communication because the optimal distance to read facial expressions in a conversation between two people is 0.8 m. Not surprisingly, arguments arise between people seating the farthest from each other.

The cozy table. Reducing table size is a way to reduce confrontation risk at the expense of cramped space.

The standing table. Allowing people to stand-up lets them free themselves from the **tyranny** of chairs.

The stand-up meeting. This layout is known to minimize meeting time[10].

[Tip 24]

Influence of layout in group IQ

Some sparse table layouts, such as the *wedding* layout increase the risk of confrontation and therefore lower the group IQ (gIQ↓). Denser layouts lead to higher gIQ↑. Above are listed four common layouts. A rule of thumb is that layouts that put distance between participants (d>2m) lead to increased miss-communication: the top source of conflict.

[10] Bluedorn, A.C., Turban, D.B. and Love, M.S., 1999. The effects of stand-up and sit-down meeting formats on meeting outcomes. Journal of Applied Psychology, 84(2), p.277.

Influence of layout in group IQ

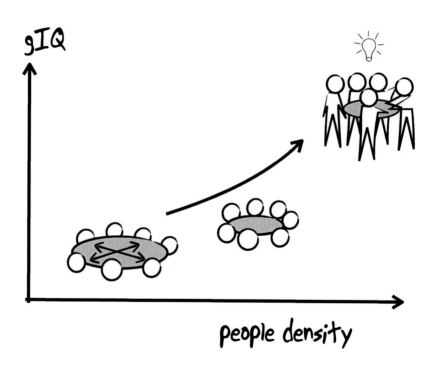

[Tip 25]

The *ideo* layout

The *ideo* layout first appeared in an episode of ABC's 1999 *Nightline* that featured Palo Alto based product design firm ideo. It is our go-to layout for whiteboard based meetings. This layout is optimal for briefings, and short presentations of fact-finding missions.

The ideo layout checklist

- ☑ Rectangular table
- ☑ If chairs are used, the chairs must have wheels
- ☑ Whiteboard close to table (d<90 cm)
- ☑ Close-pack seating arrangement (cozy)
- ☑ One person at a time uses the whiteboard
- ☑ No hoarding of table space with personal items
- ☑ No elbows on table

Note on use of a table

Recent findings suggest that layouts consisting of chairs and whiteboards but <u>without</u> table help teams think out of the box quicker than those that use tables[11].

[11] *First Class with Tina Seelig, episode five, NHK World, March 2017*

The 'ideo' layout

Designate a *room master*

Good meetings have a *facilitator*[12] (**F**) who usually guides the team through an agenda. However, **great** meetings, in addition to a facilitator, designate a so-called **host**[13] or **room master (M)**. The role of the room master is to take care of the logistics so that the *facilitator* can focus on his job.

The room master's checklist

- ☑ Table, marker size check
- ☑ 'Partie' is in place
- ☑ Noise in the room is controlled
- ☑ Lighting is appropriate (avoid poor CIR light)
- ☑ No dead zones
- ☑ The room is on schedule

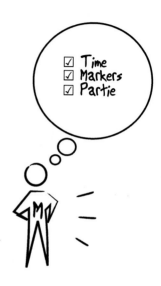

A room master is the absolute authority of a room. One of their main tasks is to keep the schedule discipline of the room. This is important if a meeting over extends its allocated time and overlaps into the next scheduled meeting. The room master is the appropriate figure if a call must be made. In upscale conferences, a room master is assigned to every room and the room master is the only one person with the authority to extend the allotted time to a facilitator. Finally, having a meeting without a room master is like going partying without a designated driver: foolish.

[12] Berengueres, J.. 2013. *The role of the facilitator, The Brown Book of Design Thinking; UAE University College.*
[13] *The host is a staple in meetings at architecture firms such as S.O.M.*

Designate a room master

How to stop the show

Time keeping is not strictly part of any layout. However, being able to stop an ongoing activity is as important as being able to start it. In a meeting, there will be times that a call or two to order might be needed. In such occasions, every facilitator has its own tricks under the sleeve. At the *d.School*, they use a big **Chinese gong**. In *Agile* workshops, they use the ***monkey call***. (In a monkey call everybody must rise both hands when they see someone rising both hands, it is a visual way for the facilitator to spread a call to order.) The drawback is that people with monkey arm syndrome don't enjoy this. Others prefer to use their own **voice**, undignified.

The bell

The brass bell on the photo is a compromise between portability and startling power. The brass produces a pure delta sound that every body seems to respect. I carry it with my key holder anywhere I go. It is the *host's* duty to provide a credible "bell" to the (visiting) facilitator.

How to stop the show

A brass crane bell is a credible show stopper.

Made in the USA
Lexington, KY
02 October 2018